COMPANY K

COMPANY K

ANDREW BROWN

ISBN: 978-93-5614-431-6

Published: 1894

LECTOR HOUSE LLP
E-MAIL: lectorpublishing@gmail.com

COMPANY K,

TWENTIETH REGIMENT,
ILLINOIS VOLUNTEER INFANTRY.

ROSTER AND RECORD

BY

ANDREW BROWN

1894

PREFACE.

At the last annual reunion of the association of the survivors of the 20th Illinois Regiment, held in Chicago September 8, 1893, I was assigned the duty of preparing a roster of Company K. This little publication is the result of my efforts to perform that duty. It is intended for the surviving members of the Company and their descendants, for relatives and friends of deceased members and for all others into whose hands it may chance to come, who are interested in learning about the men who fought and won battles that secured to America liberty and union.

ANDREW BROWN.

Newark, Illinois, June, 1894.

CONTENTS

ROSTER AND RECORD.

REUBEN F. DYER, M. D., Ottawa, Ill.

Born at Strong, Franklin county, Maine. Volunteered at Newark, Ill., April 15, 1861. Was elected Captain. Commanded Company at Fredericktown, Fort Henry and Fort Donelson. Resigned commission as Captain of Company K March 13, 1862, at Pittsburg Landing, Tennessee, with view of obtaining a position in the line of his profession. August 25, 1862, was commissioned Surgeon, 104th Regiment, Illinois Volunteer Infantry, which commission he held till close of war, and, at close was acting Medical Director 14th Army Corps, General Jefferson C. Davis commanding. Has practiced medicine at Ottawa since 1865. For a number of years a member of U. S. Board Examining Surgeons. Is not a pensioner. A republican. A Methodist.

BENJAMIN OLIN, Joliet, Ill.

Born in State of New York. Volunteered at Newark, Ill., in April, 1861. Elected Orderly Sergeant of Company. May, 1861, commissioned First Lieutenant. Served with Company in Missouri till November, 1861, when he resigned on account of ill health. Has been in the practice of law since 1862. At present County Judge of Will county, Ill. Is not a pensioner. Has never applied for a pension. A liberal democrat. A Methodist.

JOHN N. BOYER, Normal, Ill.

Born in Centre county, Pennsylvania. Volunteered May 10, 1861, at Newark, Ill. Discharged February 15, 1864, on account of wound received at Vicksburg. Was appointed Orderly Sergeant June 13, 1861. Commissioned 2d Lieutenant January 22, 1862; Captain March 13, 1862.

AT SHILOH.

On April 6, 1862, had mumps very badly, and had neck wrapped with red flannel. Nevertheless, went out in command of the Company. Had sword struck by a missile and bent nearly double, and received two slight wounds in the face. At noon was compelled to retire from the Company. When going, several of the boys turned over their pocket-books to him for safe keeping. Joined us, and took command of the Company, at daylight the next morning and was in all the second day's fighting.

AT BRITTON'S LANE.

On September 1, 1862, was indisposed and was riding in an ambulance with Assistant Surgeon Bailey and Chaplain Button. When first shots were heard at Britton's Lane he jumped out, buckled on his sword and asked Dr. Bailey to give him a strong dose of whisky and quinine and then went forward on a run to take charge of the Company. This is a true story, because Chaplain Button tells it.

AT VICKSBURG.

On May 22, 1863, while in command of the Company at Vicksburg he was shot in the foot. On this occasion he lost his sword that had been battered at Shiloh; also, most of his other personal effects. He was discharged on account of this wound and receives pension therefor at the rate of twenty dollars a month.

A MAN OF PEACE.

Since war has been teacher, farmer, business man and cattle man in the West. Is broken in health. Rheumatism and other debilities. Says he can't work much. We understand he does not have to. In one sense of the word it is supposed he is well-heeled, although in another sense it is certain he is very badly heeled. In religion a Methodist; in politics a radical republican.

PERRY W. SPELLMAN, Fellowship, Florida.

Born in Pittsford, Monroe county, New York. Volunteered April 24, 1861, at Newark, Ill. Mustered out July 16, 1865, by reason of close of war. Was appointed Sergeant in May, 1861. Detailed on recruiting service from December, 1861, to June, 1862. Was Orderly Sergeant for a few months, then reduced to the ranks and detailed as acting Hospital Steward and dispenser of medicine. Was commissioned First Lieutenant March 2, 1863, and Captain February 23, 1865.

On May 12, 1863, during our desperate struggle behind the rail fence at Raymond, Comrade Spellman had the command of the Company. Near the close of that battle, when our lines were advancing through the woods, he was hit in the side by a bullet and disabled for a time. From May 22, 1865, he commanded the Company during the siege of Vicksburg, and continued in command till the latter part of the siege of Atlanta. Was on detached service as acting assistant Quartermaster 3d Division 17th Army Corps, from October, 1864, till final muster out.

Since the war has mostly followed business pursuits. Has lived in Illinois, in South Dakota, and is now in Florida. On December 25, 1893, he wrote thus: "I came to Florida in January, 1890, and will probably spend the remainder of my days here. The climate is much more agreeable to me than that of the chilly North. Roses in full bloom and fresh vegetables for the table all winter." Pensioned for disability incurred in the army.

FAAGUST ANDERSON,

Westport, Brown County, South Dakota.

May, 1861-August 1, 1862. Born in Sweden. Came to America in 1852. Twenty years old when enlisted. Was shot in wrist at Shiloh and discharged because of wound. Enlisted in another regiment in August, 1863, and mustered out in December, 1865, on account of close of war. Is pensioned at rate of ten dollars a month for wound received at Shiloh, and other disabilities. Has been farming since the war. Is a republican, but not a church member.

CHARLES BACON,

Clinton, Oneida County, New York.

April, 1861-July, 1865. Born in Paris, Oneida county, New York. Thirty-three years old when enlisted. Pensioned at rate of eight dollars a month for disability incurred in army. Pension granted December, 1893. Votes the republican ticket as often as he has a chance to do so, but in religion is not very particular. Just goes to whatever church is handiest.

JAMES BARROWS, Newark, Ill.

April, 1861-July 24, 1862. Born in Perry, Wyoming county, New York. Was twenty-six years old when enlisted. Pensioned at twelve dollars a month. Is a painter. A member of Baptist church. A republican. Was in the ranks of Company K at Fredericktown, Fort Henry, Fort Donelson and Shiloh.

MARTIN BISSELL, Plano, Ill.

May, 1861-October 3, 1862. Born in Addison county, Vermont. Twenty-one years old when enlisted. Slightly wounded at Fort Donelson. At Shiloh was struck with fragment of bursting shell Sunday morning, in region of hip, while regiment was executing a retreat after first engagement with the enemy. Soon afterwards was struck in thigh with spent ball, and later in the battle had part of right thumb nail knocked off and bayonet scabbard cut by another ball. At Britton's Lane was shot in right shoulder; was discharged because of this wound, and draws pension therefor at the rate of eight dollars a month. Since discharged has been engaged in agricultural and mechanical pursuits. A republican. A Methodist.

ANDREW BROWN, Newark, Illinois.

April, 1861-July 14, 1864. Born of Irish parents, in Kendall county, Ill. Seventeen years old when enlisted. Did not go with Company from Newark to Joliet on Saturday, May 11, 1861, because, on that morning, clothes and other necessaries were missing, but the next day, being fairly equipped, he started on foot for Camp Goodell, east of Joliet, at 10 o'clock a. m. and reached destination at 4 p. m. Was farther away from home then than he had ever been before in his life. Had made a march of nearly thirty miles in six hours, but was in very "light marching order." Was not encumbered with a single superfluous article. When he reported in camp, Lieutenant Watson ordered the Company to form ranks and then called for three cheers for the boy they left behind them. From the day he left home till he returned, a period of more than three years, this volunteer never slept in a bed nor sat at a table to eat a meal of victuals. Was never on detailed duty, never straggled from the ranks and, while a soldier, never missed a march, campaign, skirmish or battle, except when wounded and a prisoner in the hands of the enemy. When long roll was beat Sunday morning at Shiloh, he had his gun off the stock and was swabbing out the barrel in a pail of water. Was under arrest and in guard house once only. Charges preferred were "committing depredations on private property." The "depredation" consisted of milking a cow in canteen. Read the New Testament through three times in the army. Has the little volume yet which Chaplain Button presented in May, 1861. It has been out in many a storm and is badly soaked and soiled. Was slightly wounded at Britton's Lane. Was shot twice through leg at Raymond and captured by the enemy. A prisoner for two months. Since discharged has been student, teacher, lawyer, farmer. Has never been greenbacker, free-silver man nor protective tariff man. Is a democrat, but has much regard and respect for prohibitionists. In religion liberal. Catholic rather than Protestant.

JOHN CAREY, Blackstone, Ill.

May, 1861-July 16, 1865. Born in Limerick, Ireland. Came to America in November, 1860. Was twenty-one years old when enlisted.

The preliminary skirmishing of an impending battle always acted like a tonic on this comrade, and he was never known to be out of condition whenever a battle was on. Was as good a soldier as ever fought under the Stars and Stripes.

Captured July 22, 1864, near Atlanta, and confined in Confederate prisons for nearly seven months. Finally escaped and reached Union lines near Wilmington, N. C., February 22, 1865. Pensioned at rate of twenty dollars a month for disabilities incurred in Andersonville Prison. Is a bachelor—to me it is an utterly unaccountable fact that so congenial a soul as John Carey should choose to live alone in life. Some girl may capture him yet. His widow would probably receive a nice pension when John is gone. Comrade Carey claims that he votes the republican ticket, although he is a true Irishman and a good Catholic. He did not reply to my letter of inquiry.

CHARLES CLAYTON,

26 Union St., Wakefield Road, Stalysbridge, Lancashire, England, Europe.

April, 1861-July 25, 1862. Born in England. Draws pension at rate of eight dollars a month for disabilities incurred in service. Enrolled at Washington, D. C., Agency. Certificate No. 411,108.

FRANKLIN CLIFFORD, Seneca, Ill.

April, 1861-July 16, 1865. Born in St. Louis, Missouri. Twenty-one years old when enlisted. Received some slight wounds. There was no discount on this comrade's fighting qualities. I remember that very distinctly. Was captured near Atlanta July 22, 1864. A prisoner seven months and ten days. Exchanged at Wilmington, N. C., March 1, 1865. Is pensioned at twelve dollars a month for disabilities incurred in service. Is a laborer. He writes thus: "I always vote the republican ticket.

I suppose I ought to be a religious man, but I am not."

ANDERSON CONNER,

No. 2219 Messanie St., St. Joseph, Missouri.

June 9, 1861-July 16, 1865. Born in Hunterdon county, New Jersey. Eighteen years old when enlisted. Wounded at Raymond and captured. Sent to Libby prison. A prisoner only seventeen days. Was then paroled and sent to St. Louis to await exchange. Remained at St. Louis nearly four months. Was then exchanged and served with Company K to close of war. Is pensioned at rate of ten dollars a month for disabilities incurred in the service. His paternal grandfather was in the Revolution and war of 1812. He says he has two big boys that might do for soldiers if they were drafted and put under guard where they could not run.

From 1867 to 1893 lived in Wisconsin; was engaged in lumbering and farming, but did not make a fortune. In June, 1893, went to Dwight, Ill.; stayed there two months, then went west to take a new start in life.

JAMES COYLE,

St. Louis, Missouri, No. 624-626 Washington Ave.

May, 1861-July 16, 1865. Was captured near Atlanta July 22, 1864, and confined in Confederate prisons. Escaped and recaptured in woods with dogs. Escaped again and succeeded in reaching the Union lines after traveling a distance of one hundred and fifty miles. Was wounded in trenches at Vicksburg. Is pensioned for wound. Was a very determined and resolute fighter in battle. Since war has been in business and has been successful. Is probably a democrat. Has a democratic name and lives in a democratic State. Did not answer my letter of inquiry. The facts here given are from previous knowledge.

Since writing the foregoing I have received a letter from this comrade. He was not mustered out with the regiment in July, but was retained in service by special order of War Department and mustered out September 26, 1865, at Louisville. Was shot through the right hand in front of Fort Hill, Vicksburg, May 21, 1863. When captured near Atlanta July 22, 1864, he was sent to Andersonville. On September 11, 1864, while in transit from Andersonville to another prison he and George Wilson of Company K escaped from the cars at midnight and were out fifteen days. Traveled at night and lay in concealment during the day. Were finally captured and confined in a common prison at Augusta, Ga., for three weeks. Was then sent to the new prison at Millen. Was there only one day when he escaped for the second time with a soldier of the Fifteenth Ohio regiment. Was out the second time only eleven days and was again captured, and again taken to Augusta; was there two days when he made a third escape with a Pennsylvania soldier. "After twenty-one days by constant night travel, we reached Sherman's army at Atlanta."

In politics a republican; in religion a Presbyterian.

JEROME B. DANN,

DeWitt, Saline County, Nebraska.

June 4, 1861-July 16, 1865. Born in Pennsylvania. Seventeen years old when enlisted. Captured near Atlanta July 22, 1864. A prisoner for several months. Escaped and recaptured in the woods. Since the war has followed contracting and building, and is at it yet to some extent. Health is quite unsatisfactory. Draws pension at rate of twelve dollars a month.—Has been connected with Congregational church for twenty years. Has always been a republican and expects to die a republican. You may live a long time yet, Jerome.

RUDOLPH FAVREAU,

West New Brighton, Richmond County, N. Y.

May, 1861-July 14, 1864. Born in Germany. Thirty-five years old when enlisted. Was the company fifer. Rudolph writes thus: "Ich bin 68 Yahre alt. Kam nach Amerika 1858, und bin ein Gartner. Ich leide an Reimatismus und kan garnicht mehr arbeiten und muss nun von meine Pension leben von $12 monathlich. Auszerdem gehöre ich zuder G. A. R. Post, No. 545, Port Richmond. Ich belange zu der Deutsche Kirche."

JOHN T. GRAY,

Blairsville, Indiana County, Pennsylvania.

April, 1861-July 14, 1864. Twenty-one years old when enlisted. Re-enlisted soon after discharge from Company K and served one year in U. S. veteran reserve corps. Is not in good health. Pensioned at rate of $4,00 a month for rheumatism contracted in the service. Since the war has done a little of a great many different things. When a boy he associated himself with the republican party in the days of Fremont and Dayton, and has never had just cause or provocation to change. Just now, December, 1893, he sees a blanked sight less cause to change his opinion than ever. In religion, a free thinker, he professes that he is not a Christian. He does not want to become a Christian and does not want to be classed as such. Has wife and happy family, owns the roof above them and lives contentedly. Has never, since his discharge, seen a single Company K man and but one man of the regiment.

SAMUEL HAGERMAN, Yorkville, Ill.

June 1, 1861-July 16, 1865. Born in Westmoreland county, Pennsylvania. Was twenty-seven years old when enlisted. At battle of Shiloh Samuel's gun was knocked to pieces by some kind of a missile. At Raymond he was shot in the shoulder and leg, and in the Georgia campaign had a finger shot off. Receives pension for wounds at rate of eight dollars a month. Member of Presbyterian church. A republican.

NICHOLAS HANSON,

Battle Creek, Ida County, Iowa.

May 8, 1861-July 16, 1865. Born in Schoharie county, New York. He says he was only seventeen years old when he enlisted. Was wounded July 21, 1864, near Atlanta. Draws pension for wounds at rate of four dollars a month. Is farming now and has been most of the time since the war. Is a Presbyterian. Votes the republican ticket under all circumstances. Is willing to support anything the party puts up. "If you or any other Company K folks are ever out this way hunt me up. I own a quarter-section farm four miles west of town in as good a country as is around Newark. I have never been able to meet you at any of the reunions, but I am always glad to get a card of invitation."

MARSHALL HAVENHILL,

Miner, Miner County, South Dakota.

Enlisted at Newark in April, 1861. July 20, 1861, was transferred to the regimental band.

GEORGE HOPGOOD,

Morton, Lewis County, Washington.

April, 1861-July 23, 1862. Born in England. Came to America in 1857. Twenty-one years old when enlisted. Is pensioned at the rate of four dollars a month for disabilities incurred in service.

Since the war has lived most of the time at Clinton, Missouri, and has worked as a stone-mason. Has gone west and taken a homestead and intends to grow up with the country. Is a "republican all the way through". In religion he is a true Christian. Adopts the grand principles of the Sermon on the Mount. Get your Bibles, turn to Matthew vii, 12, and read the rule that he lives by. That is good religion, George. None better was ever formulated. Live right up to it and you need have no fear of torment or torture in the life beyond this life.

EDWIN HOWES,

Eola, DuPage County, Illinois.

April, 1861-July 15, 1865. Born in State of New York. Twenty-two years old when enlisted. Wounded and captured at Britton's Lane. Paroled. Captured again near Atlanta, July 22, 1864, and sent to Confederate prisons. Escaped from prison and reached Union lines near Wilmington, North Carolina, February, 1865. Pensioned at the rate of twelve dollars a month for disabilities incurred in the service. Is a farmer. A prohibitionist. Professes to be a Christian.

Dr. WILLIAM H. H. HUTTON,

Surgeon U. S. Marine Hospital Service, Detroit, Mich.

Born in York, Jefferson county, Ohio. Enlisted in Company K, 20th Illinois regiment, June 17, 1861, at the age of twenty-three years; discharged therefrom August 28, 1862, for deafness caused by concussion of cannon at battle of Pittsburg Landing. Had participated in all battles in which Company was engaged up to date of discharge.

September 2, 1862, enlisted in Company D, 104th regiment Illinois volunteers. Reported to his Company at Louisville, Ky., October 2, 1862. Appointed Sergeant April 10, 1863. Appointed Color-Sergeant on battlefield of Chicamauga September 20, 1863. Wounded at battle of Missionary Ridge November 25, 1863. On account of disabilities was sent to Chicago, Ill., March, 1864. Was chief clerk Desmarres eye and ear military hospital, Chicago, from July 4, 1864, to March 8, 1865, at which date was discharged from 104th Illinois regiment by order of Secretary of War. Was appointed Hospital Steward U. S. A. March 8, 1864 in which capacity he served till April 1, 1871, thus making a military record of ten years. As Hospital Steward, U. S. A., he served at the following places: Chicago, Ill.; Montgomery, Mobile, and Forts Gaines and Morgan, Alabama; Charleston, S. C.; Newbern and Raleigh, N. C.; Key West and Dry Tortugas, Florida. September 8, 1871, was appointed Hospital Steward in U. S. Marine Hospital, Mobile, Alabama; resigned July 4, 1874.

Graduated from Chicago Medical College March 16, 1875. May 8, 1875, was appointed Assistant Surgeon U. S. Marine Hospital service. This appointment was made on results of competitive examination. Promoted to Surgeon October 5, 1876. As a United States medical officer has served at ports of New York, Cincinnati, Mobile, Key West, New Orleans, Baltimore, and is now serving second tour at Detroit.

Has served as Medical Inspector of the Life-Saving Service, is on several examing boards, and has had a great deal to do with National quarantine matters, especially as regards yellow fever and cholera. On one occasion represented the authority of the United States for several months, in quarantine matters, on the entire Florida coast.

This is a very brief summary of Comrade Hutton's life for nearly thirty-three years.

JAMES JENNINGS,

Sheridan, LaSalle County, Ill.

April, 1861-July 16, 1865. Born in state of New York. Twenty-one years old when enlisted. Was one of the very first to volunteer at Newark; probably signed the roll April 15, 1861. He also re-enlisted for another three years as soon as he had an opportunity to do so, which was December 16, 1863. Is well charged with grit. Was shot in shoulder at Britton's Lane. Was captured July 22, 1864, near Atlanta, and sent to Andersonville; made three escapes from prison; first and second were unsuccessful; was recaptured both times in the woods, after traveling many nights and undergoing great hardships. Third escape proved successful. Reached Union lines near Wilmington, N. C, Feb. 22, 1865. Is pensioned at rate of four dollars a month for wound received at Britton's Lane. Is a farmer. Non-sectarian in religion; republican in politics.

Comrade Jennings has been greatly bereaved by the loss of his wife who died at South San Diego, Cal., April 14, 1894. He and daughter Edith accompanied her to the Pacific coast during the preceding autumn, vainly attempting to save her from the fatal malady to which she finally succumbed. Our comrade's home is now desolate.

ELIAS KILMER,

Prophetstown, Whiteside County, Ill.

April 24. 1861-July 14, 1864. Born in Oswego county, New York. Twenty-one years old when enlisted. September 5, 1864, enlisted in 146th Regiment, Illinois Volunteers, and was discharged therefrom July 5, 1865, by reason of the termination of the war. Is pensioned at rate of six dollars a month. Since the war has been a farmer. This is the way Elias writes: "Politics, black republican. In regard to religion, my wife belongs to the Methodist church. I suppose you preached prohibition and voted democratic." There are very many republicans of my acquaintance whom I would be glad to see preaching prohibition although they continue to vote the republican ticket. No class of American citizens would be more greatly blessed and benefitted by prohibition than republicans.

JOHN LEACH, Morris, Ill.

April, 1861-July 16, 1865. Born in West Virginia. Twenty-two years old when enlisted. A carpenter. A very active republican—never preaches prohibition. Is a christian, but has not worked at the trade for many years. Did not answer my letter, and am unable to give further facts from memory.

JAMES B. LITTLEWOOD,

Washington, D. C., No. 415, B Street, N. E.

April, 1861-July, 1865. Born in England. Was struck, I think, by a spent ball at Britton's Lane. Was a good soldier. Since war, has held clerical positions in Washington; is now in the Patent Office. While performing clerical duty, studied medicine and graduated from Medical College at Georgetown, D. C. Owns a home in Washington. Is probably a democrat at the present time. Did not answer my letter of inquiry.

JOHN P. MULLENIX, Fairfield, Iowa.

May, 1861-March 25, 1862. Born in Ohio. Thirty-six years old when enlisted. Receives pension at rate of thirty dollars a month for disability incurred in service; has drawn pension from date of discharge. Badly crippled; cannot go without crutches; has no use of left arm and shoulder; rheumatism is the main difficulty. Is a Presbyterian in belief, and a republican from principle.

ALBERT PIERSON,

10 Prospect Street, East Orange, New Jersey.

June 3, 1861-November 20, 1862. In 1863, when Confederate army came up into Pennsylvania, enlisted in a militia company, and served thirty days. Born in Orange, N. J. Was twenty-two years old when enlisted. Had the pleasure of participating in only one battle during the war—that of Fredericktown, Missouri. About November 1, 1861, became very sick at Bird's Point, Missouri. On the 20th of that month received furlough and went to Mr. Jessup's, Na-au-say township, Kendall county, Illinois, where he remained for six months a very sick man. In May, 1862, was sent to East Orange, N. J., his former home, in charge of a personal attendant, and came near dying on the journey. Remained at East Orange, sick, for four months. In August reported to hospital, on Bedloe Island, from which he was discharged November 20, 1862, and it is the regret of Comrade Pierson that he was not with Company K, 20th Illinois Regiment, during the whole war. Since discharged he has been seriously sick, and has paid out money to doctors. "Yet, I believe there is One above who rules over all, and when my time comes no doctor can save me." (Doctor Taylor, what think you of this?) Comrade Pierson is a Presbyterian. He is not a pensioner; he has never applied for pension. He is a republican; is a powerful republican, and is in grief because of the ascendancy of the democratic party. This is the way he writes: "O, what a great big humbug Grover is, anyway; he ought to be in England, not America. I recall the night after the election; I expected nothing from New Jersey—she has always been a democrat—but I did expect good news from the Prairie state. At twelve o'clock report came, 'Illinois is against Harrison.' At first I refused to believe it. I had been proud of Illinois up to that time, as I had spent some years there, but now I am in sorrow for her." Albert, I am surprised that a grave and serious man of mature years would sit up till twelve o'clock watching election returns. Don't do it again. Retire at nine o'clock regularly the night after election and in the morning you will be in better condition to hear the news. You may get bad news next time, too. As ordered by the people, so will the result be.

Comrade Pierson has been engaged in different lines of business since the war—is now, and has been for some years, in the wood and coal business. He gives this cordial invitation: "If any Company K boys ever come East, I want them to run out to Orange and see me; about fourteen miles from New York City, and trains run all the time. Remember!"

In a subsequent letter, Comrade Pierson has given additional facts concerning himself. In the spring of 1857 he went out to Illinois to be a farmer. Was in Kendall county, Illinois, when the affair took place at Fort Sumpter in Charleston Harbor, and immediately joined a Company that was started at Oswego. That Company was unfortunate in not being accepted, and he was obliged to go back to work. In the meantime a Kendall county Company was organized at Newark and went into camp at Joliet. Some of the Oswego boys went to Joliet and joined that Company and sent back word that a few more men would be received. Comrade Pierson was full of the war, but was reluctant about quitting work again. One day he was plowing. His team consisted of a free horse and a very lazy one. He talked a great deal to the lazy horse and pelted him with chunks of dirt, but all this was unavailing and he decided to resort to harsher means. He stopped, threw the lines from his shoulders, swung them around the plow handle and went up alongside of the lazy animal to thrash him. But as soon as he commenced operations the free horse jumped and away went the team. After considerable time he caught them. He then felt very gritty and resolved to be a soldier. He tied the horses to a fence and started. As he passed the house he called at the door and said, "Good bye! I am off for the war," and moved on toward Joliet. On this journey he was troubled by the thought that he was liable to be rejected, as he was a small man and, at that time, first-class war material was in great abundance. When, however, he reached camp he passed muster successfully and was happy. Comrade Pierson closes his letter thus: "When another election comes 'round I want you fellows out there to attend to business better than you did before. Watch New Jersey next time."

WILLIAM PRENTICE,

Soldiers' Home, Quincy, Illinois.

Enlisted in April, 1861; served for several months in Company K. Was discharged for disability, and afterwards enlisted in another Regiment. Is a pensioner.

WILLIAM PRESTON, Steward, Illinois.

April 24, 1861-July 16, 1865. Born in Kendall county, Illinois. Twenty-one years old when enlisted. Receives pension for disability incurred in service. After war, engaged in farming; later was in business; now somewhat retired. Is interested in Company K matters, and is glad that a roster is likely to be made up.

JAY DELOS PRUYN, Oneonta, New York.

May 1, 1861-July 14, 1864. Born at Syracuse, N. Y., Twenty-two years old when enlisted. Is granted pension at rate of twelve dollars a month. Is painter and decorator. Republican. Presbyterian.

I am under special obligation to Comrade Pruyn for aiding me while lying helpless and in danger of bleeding to death on the battlefield at Raymond. He bandaged my wounded leg with his big red handkerchief, knotted and drawn very tightly, and with my own suspenders; gave me a good drink out of his canteen, and then resumed his place in the ranks. Comrade Pruyn was a good soldier, a conscientious man, a man of many good qualities. My association with him in the army will continue a pleasant recollection.

NARCISSE REMILLARD,

Mount Taber, Multnomah County, Oregon.

April 1861-July 14, 1864. September 5, 1864, enlisted in 146th Regiment, Illinois Volunteer Infantry, and was discharged therefrom July 5, 1865. Was born at Naperville, Canada. Twenty-six years old when enlisted. Is pensioned at rate of ten dollars a month for disability incurred in service. In religion, Protestant; a member of Baptist church. In politics, non-partisan. Votes with reference to the good of the country. Does not consider the interests of politicians. That is correct; vote as you shot—for country and for right.

WARREN ROCKWOOD, Sheridan, Illinois.

April, 1861-November 15, 1861. Born in state of New York. Twenty-three years old when enlisted. Receives pension at rate of eight dollars a month. Was a farmer for a number of years; now works as carpenter. Republican. Non-sectarian in religion.

BERDETTE SPENCER,

Elmira, New York, No. 1024 College Avenue.

May 13, 1861-July 14, 1864. Born at Mohawk, Herkimer county, N. Y. Thirty-three years old when enlisted. Was wounded in left forearm at Fort Donelson, and receives pension of ten dollars a month because of wound. On account of this wound he was away from the Company on furlough seven months, three months at Marine hospital, Chicago, and four months at home. During this time missed Shiloh and Britton's Lane; was in all other battles with the Company. Is now, and has been since July 24, 1876, employed at New York State Reformatory, which has about fifteen hundred prisoners. Has never seen a Company K man since the war. Wants to get all the news about the boys. Would like to attend a reunion and see them all once more. Does not know whether to call them boys now or not. Is not a church member; in belief, a spiritualist.

RICHARD SPRINGER,

Chicago, Ill., No. 99 Washington Street.

April, 1861-August 31, 1865. Born at LaFayette, Indiana. Seventeen years old when enlisted. Shot in right arm July 21, 1864, near Atlanta, while attempting to rescue Martin Morley, the regimental standard bearer, who lay wounded between the lines. Draws pension for this wound at rate of seventeen dollars a month. Since war has been student, journalist, man of affairs, engaged in various business enterprises, now handles real estate in Chicago. Fearless and aggressive in politics, as upon battlefields, he has never winced under stroke of party lash. Has been liberal republican and greenbacker. Now looks with favor upon the independent populist movement. In religion, liberal. Protestant rather than Catholic.

JOHN J. TAYLOR, M. D., Streator, Illinois.

June 17, 1861-June 16, 1862. Born in Kent, England. Came to America in 1852 with his parents when eleven years old. Came on ship Prince Albert with five hundred emigrants; thirty-seven days on sea. Has renounced allegiance to the British crown. Is now American through and through. Was twenty years old when enlisted. Receives pension at rate of eight dollars a month for disabilities incurred in service. Suffered for about twenty years after discharged from the army with alimentary and other difficulties. After coming home badly wrecked he attended Normal University with the purpose of preparing for a teacher, but was compelled by ill health to abandon the project. Began the study of medicine for personal benefit, afterwards adopted it as a profession. Studied medicine at University of Michigan in 1865-6, and in 1866-7 in Chicago at the Rush. Graduated from Rush Medical College January 25, 1867, and has since been engaged in the practice of the profession. Is a railroad surgeon, is secretary of LaSalle county Medical Society, and is examining surgeon for a number of life insurance companies. Has been president of North Central Medical Association. Has been captain of State Militia and alderman fourth ward, Streator.

This comrade is a very zealous adherent of the republican party; he has great faith in the party. He thinks the republican party is right. He thinks it always has been right. He thinks it will soon again have control of the affairs of the government. We are in great danger of being deluged by foreign goods from which calamity the government should protect us.

In religion he is broad and free. Is not priest-ridden. He cordially recognizes whatever of good there is in the "religious societies" and spreads the wide mantle of charity over all their errors. Is very willing and very anxious to learn in regard to the great beyond, but is not willing to take bit and be reined by priest or prelate. Desires liberty in regard to religious thought and action.

"Be industrious, be honest, be clean, be true to yourself and charitable to others, and lift like a Hercules to lighten the burden of those who are heavily loaded and weary in the journey of life. These things are religion." — Taylor.

"The practice of moral duties without a belief in a Divine law-giver, and without reference to His will or commands, is not religion." — Webster.

Who shall decide when doctors disagree?

WILLIAM TODD,

Illinois Soldier's Home, Quincy, Illinois.

April, 1861-May 25, 1865. Was born in Kirkcaldy, Scotland, but left the bleak, barren hills of his native land in 1849 and came to Chicago. Was twenty-nine years and nine months old when enlisted. Captured near Atlanta, Ga., July 22, 1864, and for many months confined in Confederate prisons.

Since putting foot upon the western continent William has been an enthusiastic American. He believes America should be protected. We should not break down the walls and allow the country to be flooded with goods from foreign shores. We want work to do and plenty of it. An idle brain is the devil's shop. Don't let the English, the Dutch or the French work for us, howsoever cheaply they offer their services. Comrade Todd is an idolator. He worships the republican party. He is wedded to his idol—let him alone.

In regard to religion, he writes this: "I am a Christian, *i. e.*, a believer in Christ and his teachings. I am not connected with any denomination, but have a leaning to the Congregational. My father was of that denomination in Scotland, the name for them there and in England being Independents." Became a Kendall county man by adoption.

"I enlisted at Champaign, Ill., April 18, 1861, but when we went into camp at Joliet that Company had four men above the maximum number, and the Kendall county Company lacked two men of the minimum number. I and another transferred ourselves from A to K, and were put on the muster roll as having enlisted in Company K April 24, 1861. So you can put me down in roster as having enlisted at Newark, Kendall county, Illinois, April 24, 1861."

Comrade Todd is badly broken in health. Right side partly paralyzed. He says he "cannot write worth a continental." Is a shoemaker. Has worked at that trade principally since the war, but has been otherwise employed and, he writes, "I finally got in here." He receives from Uncle Sam at Washington a regular remittance at the rate of six dollars a month. I should think the old fellow could do a little better than that.

SAMUEL TRENTOR, Morris, Illinois.

April 24, 1861-July 14, 1864. Born at Moundsville, West Virginia. Nearly nineteen years old when enlisted. Sam thought that with his long arms he could do good work with a cavalry sabre, and did not re-enlist in the 20th Regiment, but when discharged therefrom joined Captain Collins' Company of the 4th Illinois Cavalry and served until the close of the war. Was shot in the neck at Britton's Lane. Receives pension at rate of twelve dollars a month for disabilities incurred in the service. Works for a living. Writes thus: "I am not a democrat. My religion I have not yet."

WILLIAM VREELAND, Maurice, Iowa.

April, 1861-July 14, 1864. Born in Hudson county, N. J. Twenty-four years old when enlisted. Receives pension at rate of eight dollars a month for disability incurred in the service. Was a farmer for several years after discharge, but the condition of his health forced him to abandon that vocation. Is now editor and proprietor of the Maurice Free Press. "A rock-ribbed republican and a Methodist. The two things go well together, you know." How would prohibition and Methodism go? Think about it brother!

AMBROSE WALLACE.

Born in England. Enlisted in April, 1861. One day while the Regiment was guarding a railroad near Charleston, Missouri, in the fall of 1861, Wallace disappeared. Returned to the Company in about two months. Said he had been captured and had been with Jeff. Thompson at New Madrid. Sunday, April 6, 1861, he deserted from the ranks on the battlefield of Shiloh and never afterwards appeared. He now lives in Tennessee. Was heard from a few months ago. At that time he was not a pensioner, but he wanted to be. As the law now stands he is barred by his record. His only recourse is to come North and employ some available Congressman to introduce and pass through Congress a special act granting him a pension. In all probability it would be vetoed during the present administration, but the Executive would be put on record as being opposed to pensions. That would be a point gained in politics. Undoubtedly it is to the interest of Ambrose Wallace to have a change.

ANDREW WEST, Cabery, Illinois.

April, 1861-November 1, 1861. Was born in state of New York. On August 8, 1862, he enlisted in the 91st Illinois Regiment, and was discharged therefrom January 2, 1863; afterwards joined a company of New York Artillery, and while in this organization was seriously wounded in leg at Petersburg, Virginia, and draws pension for wound. Did not reply to my letter of inquiry.

I was sick of measles in a hospital at Cape Girardeau, Missouri, in September, 1861. At the same time Andrew West was very sick in another hospital close to the river. One evening, when convalescent and on the outlook for a boat upon which to return to the Regiment at Bird's Point, I sat beside Comrade West for nearly an hour and I thought every breath would be his last. The Surgeon in charge said he was dying and called an attendant, and directed him to remain with the patient, and gave the attendant specific instructions in regard to what he should do when the patient was dead. This attendant was Charles Halbert of the 7th Illinois Regiment. The end did not come as soon as anticipated, and as the attendant sat watching and waiting he reached for a sponge in a dish of water near by, squeezed it out, and with the wet sponge commenced to rub the dying man. After a little he fancied it gave relief. He continued the process of rubbing the whole body, and soon became certain that his patient was coming back to life. In the morning Andrew West was in a greatly improved condition and the doctor was astonished.

Why did not the dying man die? Comrade Pierson would say it was because his time had not yet come. Charles Halbert says he saved him.

ALONZO WHITE, Saunemin, Illinois.

June 11, 1861-July 16, 1865. I saw Comrade White about six years ago. At that time he was a Methodist, a prohibitionist and was not a pensioner. He had never applied for pension and never expected to apply. I do not know whether he has held out faithfully up to the present time or not on all these points. He did not reply to my letter of inquiry. I wrote to the postmaster of his town and got this: "Yes, he is here. He runs a blacksmith shop in this town."

ANDREW JACKSON WILSEY, Aurora, Illinois.

April, 1861-June 9, 1862. Born in Madison county, New York. Twenty-one years old when enlisted. Since discharge has followed a diversity of pursuits. He is not a pensioner but, I think, would not object to being enrolled as one of Uncle Sam's beneficiaries. I meet him frequently. He has never given serious thought to religion and, I understand, has no well defined and settled theological opinions. In politics he is a democrat, a regular old-fashioned democrat of the Andrew Jackson type. He was not at New Orleans, however, but he faced fury of shot and shell at

Shiloh.

DeWITT C. WILSON, Plattville, Illinois.

June 11, 1861-July 14, 1864. Born in Shelby county, Ohio. Nineteen years old when enlisted. Is not a pensioner. Since the war has been a farmer. In politics a straight republican. In religion aims to be a practical christian. He believes that good works are more efficacious than loud prayers and soul-saving sermons. He has no connection with any religious sect.

On the morning of June 11, 1861, his father sent him into a field with a horse to cultivate corn with a shovel plow. After working a few hours he tied his horse to a fence at one end of the field and started directly to Joliet on foot to enlist. He did good work as a soldier for more than three years.

All will have a vivid recollection of Fort Donelson. The lack of rations, the lack of tents or protection of any kind, the hard fighting and the hard weather, the rain, the sleet, the snow, the cold, the long dreary nights without fires. On one of those nights DeWitt Wilson and the writer stood on picket guard together close up to the enemy's works. We were posted stealthily after dark under a low bushy tree near a road which led to and from the town. We were to remain very quiet, not to speak louder than a whisper, and to watch closely all night. If the enemy sallied out in force we were to fire and run to the Regiment. It was very cold. The mercury was going down and was not far from zero. Our clothes had been soaked by previous rains and were now frozen stiff and clanked with every movement. We remained as posted for several hours. Finally, the Confederates came over their works and made a vigorous assault with intent to break the Union line. When the assault was made I was in an almost helpless condition. I could scarcely move and was nearly captured. I and my comrade became separated. I lost my course and went into the 11th Illinois Regiment. DeWitt and I frequently refer to that terrible night, the hardest in all our experience.

At Britton's Lane Comrade Wilson and two others occupied a slight ambuscade. He was very anxious to have the enemy show up, and poked his cap out on the end of his ramrod. Just as he did this a glancing bullet struck the side of his head and caused him to roll over two or three times. His face and clothes were smeared with blood, and just then he would not be considered a good-looking man.

GEORGE WILSON,

Sharon Springs, Wallace County, Kansas.

"Sharon is like a wilderness." —Isaiah 33: 9.

April, 1861-July 16, 1865. Was born at Newark, Illinois, April 5, 1838. Twenty-three when enlisted. Was wounded in hand at Britton's Lane. Was captured near Atlanta, July 22, 1864, and confined in various Confederate prisons for nearly nine months. Pensioned for disabilities incurred in service at rate of four dollars a month. Is a "homesteader" in Western Kansas, seven miles from the Colorado line.

"I belong to the prevailing church and I vote as I shot—against the South." "Cease firing! They have surrendered!" The men of the Twentieth heard those words on many battle fields. Finally they all surrendered and grounded arms. We whipped the rebels. We whipped them thoroughly. The entire South lay prostrate and bleeding and helpless at the feet of the conquering soldiers of the Union. Now, George, come out from the "prevailing church," the big wicked church of the world, and be a christian. Forgive your enemies and conquer by kindness. Bless them that curse you. Do good to them that despitefully use you and persecute you and say all manner of evil against you falsely. This is the true way. Consider these thoughts seriously, and when you vote again think of something else besides voting against the South.

JOSIAH WRIGHT,

Akron, Washington County, Colorado.

April, 1861-August 9, 1862. Born in Luzern county, Pennsylvania. Twenty-two years old when enlisted. Was a non-commissioned officer and member of the color guard. Was shot through right wrist while bearing aloft the flag of the 20th Regiment at Shiloh. Was discharged because of wound. Pensioned for wound at rate of sixteen dollars a month.

Lived in Pennsylvania till 1851. From 1851 to 1871 lived in Kendall county, Illinois. From 1871 till 1892 lived in Adair county, Missouri. From spring of 1892 to present time has lived on a homestead in Washington county, Colorado. Is now, and always has been, a farmer.

In religion is a Methodist. In politics has been a populist since the date of the organization of that party. Frequently advocates the principles of the party from the rostrum. Is very friendly to silver. On his envelopes he has the motto: "Silver sixteen to one." I think Jo has a silver mine on his homestead in Colorado.

Here is a vivid picture from Josiah Wright's pen which every man of the 20th Regiment who was on hand at Shiloh will appreciate: "I was at the spring in camp Sunday morning, April 6. The roar of the assault on General Prentis's division had become terrific. I heard drums beat the long roll as the signal of alarm. I rushed to the Colonel's tent and got the flag. In passing out I met the Color Sergeant and gave the flag to him. The boys of the 20th were swarming out of their tents with their guns. The Regiment was quickly formed and started on a run in the direction of the firing. Colonel Marsh rode rapidly up and down the column urging the men to their utmost. We did not have to go far. The Confederates were advancing with great impetuosity and sweeping the field before them. We took position to beat back the on-coming tide and then the flag was unfurled and waved in the face of the foe. The Color Sergeant was immediately shot down. I picked up the flag and was soon wounded. Another member of the color guard then took the flag. I was sent to a boat on the river and was nearly gone from loss of blood."

This also from Comrade Wright's letter: "As I write grave thoughts crowd in upon me. I go back in memory to the days of '61. I am again at the war meeting in Newark, where I listened to the thrilling eloquence of Watson until fired by a new born purpose I there resolved to serve my country and, if so it be ordered, to die in the service. I was one of the first to sign the Company roll. We are now widely scattered, but are bound together by the strongest ties. We will hardly meet again in this life, but may we so live that we shall meet around our Father's throne where severed ties of earth shall be re-united in Heaven." To this closing sentiment of our brave Comrade say I, most heartily, Amen. So may we live. Let every Company K man, still left, use this prayer. Comrades Gray and Taylor, join in.

OUR RECRUITS.

TWO SPLENDID ENGLISHMEN.

On the 4th of July, 1861, two young men of good appearance walked into our camp and immediately declared their intentions. They proposed to unite with us. We cordially accepted, and the next day the ceremony was performed.

JOHN BROAD,

Schell City, Vernon County, Missouri.

July 5, 1861-November 27, 1861. Born in England. Came to America in 1859. Twenty-two years old when enlisted. Pensioned at rate of four dollars a month for disabilities incurred in service. A carpenter by trade, but now farming. Was brought up an Anglican. At present a member of the M. E. church, South. Formerly a democrat. Now votes with the Alliance.

THOMAS HOPGOOD,

Clinton, Henry County, Missouri.

July 5, 1861-July 5, 1864. Born in England. Came to America May, 1859. Twenty-six years old when enlisted. Receives no pension. Politics, republican all the time. Religion, Protestant, a Presbyterian. Has not forgotten the time when we campaigned together. Remembers all the boys and wants to be remembered by all of them.

TWO MORE RECRUITS, BUT NOT OF A KIND.

About the middle of August, 1861, two large and very brave looking men, Bishop and another[1], came down from Kendall county, Illinois, to join Company K. We were then at Cape Girardeau, Missouri, and just at that juncture were in need of re-inforcements. A Confederate army under General Polk had crossed the river at Columbus, Kentucky, and was threatening the town. When the recruits arrived the camp was in commotion on account of the expected attack. Bishop immediately got a gun, took his place in the ranks and was ready for active hostilities. The other became sad and pensive. He did not want a gun, and did not appear so much of a warrior as at the moment of his arrival. He finally went on board of a boat with some women and children and crossed the Mississippi river. After remaining in the woods of Southern Illinois for a few days he came back to camp to

[1] In original manuscript the name of this recruit was given, but it is here omitted in compliance with the very earnest solicitation of the printer.

get his carpet bag. He did not want to be mustered into the army. He wanted to go to his peaceful home, and he went. He still lives in Illinois. I am not informed as to whether he has succeeded in getting a pension or not. His case will require a special act.

LEWIS G. BISHOP, Grand Junction, Colorado.

July 16, 1861-August 9, 1862. Born in Yorkshire, Cattaraugus county, New York, on St. Patrick's day, 1838. Was, therefore, twenty-three years old at time of enlistment. Was wounded in left arm and left leg at Shiloh. Was sent down the rivers to hospitals at Paducah and Mound City. In course of time obtained leave of absence and went up to Newark, Illinois. Was then made aware that the people appreciated the soldiers. Was lionized wherever he went in Kendall county, which was a source of embarrassment to him, as he was a modest and humble individual. Was discharged because of wounds and receives pension therefor at rate of twelve dollars a month. He is glad that he still has his left leg, although it is not as good as the other. He is obliged to wear a rubber stocking and use other appliances to suppress inflammation and reduce varicose veins.

Comrade Bishop remembers with minute particularity the events of the Fort Henry and Fort Donelson campaigns. He remembers as though it were yesterday the morning, when, at dawn, we discovered lines of Confederates looking at us from their rifle pits and when Chaplain Button went upon his knees on the ground and prayed with great earnestness for the salvation of the souls of those who should be slain in the impending battle. He thinks that if the Chaplain had taken a fife and stepped out and played "Yankee Doodle" it would have a better effect. He confesses that the prayer depressed him. In the state of mind in which he was at that time he would greatly prefer to live than to die and take his chances for heaven. This was probably the prevailing sentiment among the soldiers of both armies.

Comrade Bishop came West in the spring of 1860; went as far as Fort Larimie, Wyoming, returned in the fall to Illinois, taught school near Newark in winter of 1860-61; in spring of 1861 went to Wisconsin and helped to run a raft of lumber out of the Wisconsin river down to Muscatine; in July, 1861, returned to Kendall county, Illinois. When the disaster occurred at Bull Run he awoke to the fact that the country was seriously menaced and resolved to be a soldier. He was acquainted with many of the boys of Company K, had visited them in Joliet, and he decided to cast his lot with them. He picked up his carpet-bag and went to Cape Girardeau, Missouri, and was mustered in.

After discharge Comrade Bishop became a student and a teacher; later he studied dentistry, and for many years has been engaged in the practice of that profession.

Religion: Agnostic. He neither asserts nor denies any theological dogma.

Politics: Anything to beat the republican party. Believes that the principles and methods of that party should be relegated to "innosuous desuetude." The party is owned and fenced in by syndicates, corporations and factories, and is not worthy of public confidence. The people should rise in their sovereign capacity and decree that capital shall cease to dominate the legislation of the country.

Comrade Bishop has been married and he has been un-married. He considers that St. Paul gave first-class advice when, in his letter to the Corinthians, he wrote, "Seek not a wife."

AUGUSTUS GAY,

No. 902 Second Street, Seattle, Washington.

April 5, 1862-April 9, 1865. Was born at Albany, New York, in July, 1846. Was, therefore, fifteen years and nine months old when he enlisted. Was the youngest man in Company K, and looked very honest. No boy in the whole Union army had a more innocent face than Augustus Gay. He came to us at Joliet and was rejected. He followed up the Regiment for about a year and during most of that time had a position on Dr. Bailey's staff. Finally, at Pittsburg Landing, the day before the battle of Shiloh, he was mustered into the service as a member of Company K. Was mustered out at Raleigh, North Carolina, by reason of the expiration of his term of enlistment.

Augustus Gay appeared to court danger. He went into battle with a broad smile on his face and a twinkle of the eye as though he were engaged in something pleasant and agreeable. Was very reckless and daring in action. The wonder was how it happened that he was never killed. Was captured near Atlanta July 22, 1864, and went to Anderson prison, where he spent several months. Was finally transferred by the Confederates from Andersonville to Savannah and was at that place when it was captured by the Union army December 21, 1864.

I am in receipt of a long and interesting letter from Comrade Gay in which he gives facts concerning himself. This is dated March 26, 1894. I had previously written him up for the roster from memory and had classed him among the missing. He says he was very glad to hear from Company K. He has never seen any of the Company since the war, and had never heard from any of them. He was not sick a day while in the army and was never wounded. Since the war he has never been so seriously sick as to be confined to his bed. He is not a rich man and he is not a poor man. He weighs 250 pounds. He lives well. He never chews nor smokes tobacco nor drinks intoxicating liquors and never plays cards. He has been on the Pacific slope for twenty years and has not been back to the States during that time. He has been married for ten years and has now a boy more than half as old as he was when he joined Company K. After the war he studied dental surgery and has followed that profession continuously. Receives pension at rate of six dollars a month. Writes thus: "I want you to put in your roster that if ever a Company K man comes to this part of the world I want him to come and see me."

He says that he is Protestant. But I don't think he is a full-blooded Protestant. If I remember correctly he used to tell us in the army that his parents were Hibernians, and that he was half Catholic and half Protestant, and had by inheritance all the good qualities of both kinds of religion.

JAMES SPRINGER,

Eighty-eighth and Throop Streets, Chicago, Illinois.

Born on a farm near La Fayette, Indiana. Enlisted August 28, 1862, at the age of twenty-two years. Joined Company K at Holly Springs, Mississippi, in November, 1862, and served until mustered out at the close of the war in 1865.

After discharge became a student at the University of Chicago, also, law department thereof, from which he graduated in June, 1868, and was then admitted to the bar. Practiced law for sixteen years. For a time was engaged in journalism. Since 1885 has followed a business career.

In politics an independent; in religion a Methodist.

LAMBERT CONNER, Braidwood, Illinois.

Born in Hunterdon county, New Jersey. I think he enlisted in the spring of 1863. Was then eighteen years old. Mustered out July 16, 1865. Receives pension at rate of sixteen dollars a month for disabilities incurred in service. He did not reply to my letter of inquiry.

FOUR KIDS.

Four nice boys, in a bunch, came into our camp at Big Black river, Mississippi, about the first of April, 1864. These were Pease Barnard, Charles Hall, Luman Preston and Fayette Scofield. They were all "Suckers," were separated from their mothers for the first time and, to the old campaigners of Fort Donelson, Shiloh and Vicksburg, they, appeared very fresh and innocent. They had been mustered in several weeks before by a recruiting officer in Illinois, and fitted out with Uncle Sam's uniforms, and were now ready to assist in winding up the war.

NATHANIEL PEASE BARNARD,

Newark, Illinois.

February 25, 1864-July 16, 1865. Born in LaSalle county, Illinois. Seventeen years old when enlisted. Served in Georgia, went with Sherman from Atlanta to the sea, and helped to eviscerate the Carolinas. Pensioned at rate of eight dollars a month. Member of M. E. church. An active member of republican party. A lawyer by profession.

CHARLES HALL,

Westport, Brown County, South Dakota.

February 24, 1864-July 16, 1865. Born in Kendall county, Illinois. Eighteen years old when enlisted. July, 1864, in Georgia campaign, was shot in the neck, and for a time was supposed to be dead. This recruit was built of good material for a soldier. Did not answer my letter.

LUMAN PRESTON, Dixon, Illinois.

February 16, 1864-July 16, 1865. Born in Kendall county, Illinois. Eighteen years old when enlisted. Is in business. Did not reply to my letter of inquiry. Is probably very busily engaged attending to customers. I meet Luman occasionally. He is always in good shape and happy. I think he is a democrat. Is of the bluest Puritan blood, but has the figure of a Teuton.

OUR MISSING MEMBERS.

The following four Company K men I cannot find. If any Comrade can give me any information concerning any of them I desire to have him do so. They may be living, but I think it is more probable that they are dead:

GEORGE ADAMS.

June, 1861-October 14, 1862. Born in England.

JOHN CONSTANTINE.

May, 1861-August 29, 1861. Born in Ireland. Came to America when one year old. Claimed to have been discharged from the regular army a short time before enlisting in Company K. Was an intemperate, boisterous and quarrelsome man. Was dismissed from the army by sentence of a court martial.

LOUIS MINTZ.

April, 1861-August 24, 1863. Born in Portugal. In religion was supposed to be a Hebrew. I think he came to Newark as a peddler and there joined Company K. He was a good soldier, but was very excitable. On one occasion, when advancing on skirmish line through the woods, he fired into a dead rebel who was hanging on a fence. Comrade Mintz was overheated at Raymond, from which he never recovered, and on account of which he was discharged.

JOHN PEPOON.

May, 1861-December 16, 1862. At time of enlistment he lived in Oswego township, Kendall county, Illinois.

OUR DEAD.

For many years earth has held the ashes of our fallen Comrades in its bosom. We have kept their memories in our hearts.

SLAIN IN BATTLE.

ANDREW WILSON, Plattville, Illinois.

Born in Ohio. Enlisted June 17, 1861, at the age of twenty-three years. Shot through the head at Fort Donelson, and instantly killed, February 15, 1862, while the Union line was advancing on the enemy.

Early on the morning of the 16th the Confederates surrendered. I was on the detail sent out that day to bury the dead of our Regiment. We went to the place where we had position in the line and there, on a hard hill, through stones and roots we dug a grave. This is the only grave I have ever helped to dig. It was thirty feet long and a little more than six feet wide. When of sufficient depth two men remained in the bottom, and others handed down, one by one, eighteen men of the 20th Illinois Regiment. Andrew Wilson was one of the number. When they had all been placed side by side across the grave, good Chaplain Button spoke solemn, earnest words in exhortation and prayer. Our dead were covered with earth, three volleys were fired over them as a parting salutation, and we then filed away into camp, weary and sad.

CURTIS WANN, Newark, Illinois.

Born in Clarion county, Pennsylvania, October 2, 1843. Enlisted in Company K, April, 1861. Shot and killed instantly in the battle of Shiloh, Sunday, April 6, 1862. I have a clear recollection of Curtis Wann on the morning of that dreadful day, when we were going forward to meet the enemy. His face was aglow with eagerness and courage, but alas! he was the first to fall.

JAMES CRELLEN, Newark, Illinois.

Born on the Isle of Man. Had not been in America many years. Was a shoe-maker, and worked at his trade in Newark. Was well thought of by everybody. He was one of the first to sign the Company roll. He said at the outset that he wanted to be killed if he could not come out of the war entire. He dreaded mutilation more than death. At Shiloh, Sunday, April 6, 1861, he was shot through the neck and killed instantly. I had my eyes squarely upon him when he was struck. He dropped to the ground and never moved. Did not even quiver. While lying dead upon the battlefield he was again shot through the face.

MARCUS MORTON.

Enlisted at Joliet May, 1861. Was shot and mortally wounded at Shiloh April 6, 1861. Died in a few days after the battle.

ISRAEL WATERS, Plattville, Illinois.

Enlisted at Joliet in May, 1861. Was shot and instantly killed May 12, 1863, in the battle of Raymond. While we were engaged in the desperate fighting behind the rail fence I turned my eyes on Waters and he was cheering and shouting defiance to the enemy. In a few moments I looked again and he lay perfectly dead. A bullet had passed through his brain.

WILLIAM SHOGER, Oswego, Illinois.

Born in Germany. Came to America in 1855. Enlisted in May, 1861, at the age of nineteen years. Shot and killed instantly in the battle of Raymond May 12, 1863. Was brought up and confirmed a Lutheran. Later withdrew from Lutheran church and became an active member of Evangelical church.

DAVID BARROWS, Newark, Illinois.

Born in New Hampshire. Enlisted April, 1861, at the age of thirty-five years. Shot and killed instantly in the battle of Raymond May 12, 1863. Was a married man and left a wife and three little girls lonely and sad. If I were asked who was the best soldier in Company K the first man I would think of would be David Barrows. He did not waste much powder. A good marksman, and level-headed under the most trying circumstances, he aimed and fired in the heat and fury of battle with the precision and accuracy of target practice.

Comrades Waters, Shoger and Barrows were at my right. They were all shot through the head and, when killed, lay touching each other.

BENJAMIN ADAMS, Newark, Illinois.

Born in Kendall county, Illinois. Enlisted April, 1861, at the age of twenty years. Killed in battle of Raymond May 12, 1863. Comrade Adams was shot at the very beginning of the battle, as we lay in the woods waiting for the skirmishers to rally in, and before we fired a gun. At the close of the battle he was still living. A comrade paused over him and said—

"Can I do anything for you?"

"No."

"Ben, you are badly hurt. Won't I stay with you?"

"They are running, are they not?"

"Yes, we have them on the run. Won't I stay with you?"

"No; go on."

He was taken by an ambulance to the field hospital and died in a few minutes after reaching that place.

HENRY MITCHELL,

Na-au-say Township, Kendall County, Illinois.

Born of English parents on Prince Edward's Island January 31, 1836. Came to Kendall county, Illinois, in 1845. Enlisted in Company K May, 1861, at the age of twenty-five years. Killed in the battle of Raymond May 12, 1863.

Henry Mitchell was in every sense a large, strong, brave man, and was highly regarded by all such as have regard for what is true and noble in human life and character. He was scrupulously correct in all his habits. Never played cards, was never profane in speech, and never had any use for whisky, tobacco or beer. He had five brothers in the Union army, all in Company C of the 7th Illinois Regiment, namely, Anthony, William, George, Robert and Samuel. These five in the 7th Regiment and Henry in the 20th were all in the battle lines at Fort Donelson and Shiloh. I do not believe that there is in the whole range of history another instance in which six brothers fought in the ranks of any army in the same great battles. I have read of Roman patriotism and Grecian valor, of Spartan mothers sending out their sons to battle with the injunction to come back either victorious or dead, but I have never read of anything that is equal to the case of the six Mitchell brothers in patriotism, devotion and valor, all of whom responded at once to their country's first call for volunteers.

Of these six brave brothers only three now survive, namely—Anthony, in Kansas, and Robert and Samuel, in Colorado. George was slain on the second day at Shiloh. "We were all within six feet of George when he fell," writes Anthony. That is, the other four of the 7th Regiment; and Henry was close by in the 20th Regiment. William contracted disease in the army, came home sick and died.

ROBERT TAYLOR, Lisbon, Illinois.

Born in England. Came to America when a child. Enlisted in Company K, April, 1861, at the age of about twenty-three years. Shot through hip and mortally wounded in battle of Raymond May 12, 1863. Lived a few days after the battle and died in extreme agony. I lay near him in the hospital. His suffering was the most terrible that I have ever witnessed.

WILLIAM READ, Newark, Illinois.

Was a recruit. I think he came to the Company in 1862. Was shot in head and mortally wounded in battle of Raymond, May 12, 1863. Lived a few days after the battle.

JOHN WOODRUFF, Oswego, Illinois.

Enlisted in May, 1861. Shot and mortally wounded in the battle of Raymond,

May 12, 1863. Was shot in leg below the knee. Three different amputations were performed, one below the knee and two above, but each was followed by unfavorable results. He and I were in the same hospital, and not very far apart. I witnessed the amputations. The patient in all his suffering exhibited the most incredible fortitude. He lived nearly three weeks and never groaned nor sighed. At last when informed that mortification was advancing and the end was near, he called an attendant, paid him for extra service rendered and then turned over to the attendant his pocket-book and some other personal effects to be sent to his sister at Iowa Falls, Iowa. This was done with perfect deliberation. He manifested no fear of death. I remember him very distinctly in former battles. He was a very brave soldier.

RICE BAXTER,

Na-au-say Township, Kendall County, Illinois.

May, 1861-October 13, 1861. In a few months after being discharged from Company K he enlisted in another Regiment and was killed in the battle of Arkansas Post, January 10, 1863. I have been unable to obtain any information concerning Comrade Baxter from any of his relatives, although I have made persistent efforts to do so.

DIED IN THE SERVICE.

THOMPSON BRISTOL, Newark, Illinois.

Enlisted in April, 1861, at the age of nineteen years. Went into camp at Joliet, became sick, went home on furlough and died June 16, 1861. Buried in Millington. Let his grave be decorated.

WILLIAM ASHTON, Lisbon, Illinois.

Born of English parents in Delaware county, Pennsylvania. Enlisted April, 1861, at the age of nearly twenty-one years. Died at Cape Girardeau, Missouri, September 2, 1861.

STEPHEN JENNINGS, Newark, Illinois.

Born in State of New York. Enlisted April, 1861, at the age of twenty-five years. Died of typhoid fever in hospital at Mound City, Illinois, October 15, 1861.

RICHARD CONNER, Plattville, Illinois.

Born in Hunterdon county, New Jersey. Enlisted June 12, 1861, at the age of twenty years. Died of measles in hospital at Mound City, Illinois, December 23, 1861.

FRANK LEHMAN.

Born in Germany. Enlisted May, 1861. Died at Bird's Point, Missouri, January 11, 1862.

JOHN R. McKEAN, Newark, Illinois.

Was one of the first to volunteer in April, 1861. Had been in the regular army and, I think, for a short time in the Mexican war. Took a very active part in organizing the Company and drilling the boys. Was elected Second Lieutenant. A very efficient officer. Died at Bird's Point, Missouri, January 23, 1862.

Does any comrade know anything about Lieutenant McKean's burial? If so, report to me, please.

GEORGE MALLORY, Newark, Illinois.

Born at Rome, Oneida county, New York, November 10, 1835. Came to Kendall county, Illinois, in 1838. Enlisted April, 1861, at the age of twenty-five years. Died at Bird's Point, Missouri, January 28, 1862.

WILLIAM CROWNER.

Enlisted in May, 1861. Died in hospital at Mound City, March 10, 1862.

EDWARD ATKINS, Newark, Illinois.

Enlisted April, 1861. Died at Newark, Illinois, March 11, 1862, while home on furlough sick.

AARON PAXSON, Newark, Illinois.

Enlisted May, 1861. Died at Newark, Illinois, May 4, 1862, while home on furlough sick.

WILLIAM BENNETT,

Adams Township, La Salle County, Illinois.

Born in England January 4, 1837. Enlisted at Newark April, 1861, at the age of twenty-four years. His vitality was overtaxed at Fort Donelson. He broke down and never recovered. Was sent down the river and died in general hospital at St. Louis, Missouri, May 5, 1862.

ALBERT WILCOX, Lisbon, Illinois.

Born in Kendall county, Illinois, January 21, 1842. Enlisted April, 1861, at the age of twenty years. Died in hospital at St. Louis, Missouri, May 13, 1862.

OTIS CHARLES, Bristol Station, Illinois.

Born in Bristol township, Kendall county, Illinois. Enlisted May, 1861, at the age of twenty-five years. Overcome by the strain at Fort Donelson he went home on furlough sick, and died at his home June 1, 1862.

WILLIAM SMITH, Plattville, Illinois.

Born in Centre county, Pennsylvania. Enlisted May, 1861, at the age of twenty years. Died at Paducah, Kentucky, August 23, 1862, while on detailed duty in the Signal Corps.

JOSEPH SPRINGER.

Born in Philadelphia, Pennsylvania, February 10, 1831. Enlisted as a recruit in Company K August 30, 1862. Died at Lake Providence, Louisiana, March 18, 1863. Was a member of the Protestant Methodist Church. Belonged to the society organized at Millbrook, Kendall county, Illinois. Was married, and when he went away to the war left at home a wife and three boys, whose respective ages were seven, five and about two and one-half years. His widow, Mrs. Ann Springer, now lives at Firth, Lancaster county, Nebraska, from whose letters I make the following extracts: "I am glad the survivors of Company K are hunting up the records of those that never returned, as well as the records of those who were spared to come back. I have been weighed down and almost crushed with sorrow and affliction. I have never re-married, and, of course, draw pension at the rate of twelve dollars a month. I have lived with my boys, the oldest of whom was taken away when nearly sixteen years of age. The other two are still spared. I had four brothers who went out to fight for the dear old flag. Two of them never returned. One was William Bennett of Company K. He responded to the first call and enlisted at Newark, Illinois, early in the spring of 1861. Another brother, who was in the artillery service, was killed in the battle of Stone River. God bless the soldiers; they did a noble work; they are the saviors of the country. If the Company K Roster is published I want a copy."

ALFRED GRISWOLD, Newark, Illinois.

Enlisted April 1861. Died at Berry's Landing, Louisiana, March 20, 1863.

SUMNER COOK, Newark, Illinois.

Enlisted April, 1861. Died at Vicksburg, Mississippi, of typhoid fever, July 20, 1863.

GEORGE SLEEZER, Newark, Illinois.

Born in Kendall county, Ill. Enlisted as a recruit for Company K September 26, 1864, at the age of eighteen years. Became sick at Camp Butler, near Springfield, Illinois, and died at that place November 13, 1864, before he reached the Company.

WALTER LANDON,
Fox Township, Kendall County, Illinois.

Volunteered as a recruit for Company K October 3, 1864, and died in a short time afterward at Camp Butler, Illinois, before reaching the Company.

GREENBURY LEACH, Lisbon, Illinois.

Born in West Virginia. Enlisted April, 1861. Captured near Atlanta, Georgia, July 22, 1864. Confined in Confederate prisons from date of capture until the following spring. Died at Fortress Monroe, Virginia, April 30, 1865, just after being exchanged and while on his way to the north. Was a member of the Methodist Episcopal church. While in the army always attended whatever religious service was conducted in camp. Was a regular attendant and participant at regimental prayer-meetings.

DIED SINCE DATE OF DISCHARGE.

NELSON DAYTON, Newark, Illinois.

Enlisted April, 1861, at the age of eighteen years. Discharged for disability November 27, 1861. Died March 4, 1862, at Newark, Illinois.

ROBERT LAWTON.

May 1861-August 17, 1862. Born in Lancashire, England. Came to America in 1852. Died in Kendall county, Illinois, of the disease for which discharged from the army April 14, 1864, at the age of twenty-five years, three months and eight days. Robert was a good soldier. I remember him distinctly on the battlefield of Shiloh. During the terrible fighting of the first day he turned over his pocket-book to a member of the Company who retired on account of wounds. He did not want his money to be taken by the rebels if he were killed in the fight.

Comrade Lawton's remains were interred in the little cemetery at Plattville. The slab marble which marks his final resting place has fallen down and is broken. When the flowers of May each year come, let patriot hands decorate this grave.

GILBERT MORTON, Oswego, Illinois.

Enlisted May, 1861. Mustered out July 16, 1865. Promoted to Quartermaster Sergeant of the Regiment at the outset and, I think, held that position during the entire war. After discharge he became a railroad official and had a highly successful career for about ten years. But evil days came, and he finally died by his own hand at a hotel in Chicago. This was about the year 1876.

LONGEN MERKLI.

Born in 1829 at Damsingan, Baden, Germany. Went into German army in his youth, and was thoroughly trained as a soldier. Participated in active warfare in 1848-'49. He handled sword and bayonet with great dexterity. Few men could stand before him with these weapons. After his service in the German army he spent several years as a student. Was a good latin scholar, and had a knowledge of the French language. Pursued a course of study in surgery and medicine in a German University, and, by members of his profession, was considered an expert anatomist. Had been reared in the faith of the Catholic church, but became a doubter of the fundamental doctrines of Christianity. Came to America in 1860 and engaged in the practice of medicine at Milford and Newark. Was one of the first to enlist in April, 1861. Served in the ranks of the Company for about a year and a half. Was in the battles of Fredericktown, Fort Donelson and Shiloh. Was shot in the foot at Shiloh. Was a remarkably brave and fearless man. About July, 1862, he was detailed to serve in a hospital at Jackson, Tennessee. When negro soldiers were enlisted he was offered a commission as assistant surgeon of a negro Regiment, but declined it. He continued on detailed duty and served as a medical man in various hospitals until the expiration of his term of enlistment. Was mustered out in July, 1864. After the war, located at Bristol, Illinois, and pursued the practice of medicine. In his best years he was unable to control his appetite for strong drink and, as time advanced, his appetite steadily increased and he became an abject slave. He died at Bristol, Illinois, August 20, 1879.

GEORGE WATSON, Newark, Illinois.

I doubt whether any man did as much as George Watson toward getting up Company K. He was a lawyer at Newark, was a democrat, voted for Bell and Everett in 1860, and was an enthusiastic Union man. He was a fluent off-hand speaker and was the main figure at all the war meetings in Newark. Had been in Pennsylvania militia and Mexican war and was a good drill master. Was elected First Lieutenant. About the first of June, 1861, he withdrew from the Company and joined Mulligan's Regiment in Chicago. Was captured with that command at Lexington, Missouri, in 1861. After this he served on a gunboat and, still later, had a commission in a Pennsylvania Cavalry Regiment. He was gifted with talent of a high order, but an uncontrollable appetite for intoxicating liquor barred all possibility of success in life. It caused his ruin and downfall and death. He made many spasmodic attempts at reformation, and at these times was a successful temperance talker. But all his efforts at reform ended in failure. From the United States Soldiers' Home at Milwaukee, Wisconsin, I have received this: "The records show that George W. Watson served in Company K, 20th Illinois Infantry; Company E, 23d Illinois Infantry; Company F, 2d Pennsylvania Cavalry, and in U. S. Navy. He was admitted here December 15, 1877, and was killed by a railroad train in Milwaukee, Wisconsin, at about 3 o'clock p. m., August 21, 1879."

FAYETTE SCOFIELD, Newark, Illinois.

Born in DuPage county, Illinois, January 25, 1847. Enlisted as a recruit for Company K February 25, 1864. Discharged July 16, 1865. Killed in a railroad wreck in Missouri February 17, 1881.

AMON HEACOX, Lisbon, Illinois.

Born in Oneida county, New York, June 6, 1817. Enlisted in Company K, May, 1861, at the age of forty-four years. Mustered out July 14, 1864. Was the oldest man in the Company. I have been informed that he was slightly wounded at Britton's Lane, but I have no recollection of it. I remember him very distinctly at Fort Donelson. He was a good man and a good soldier. Was a member of M. E. church. Was one of six, many years ago, to organize a Methodist Episcopal church in Lisbon,

Illinois. He died in the Soldiers' Home at Quincy, Illinois, April 23, 1889, in the seventy-third year of his age. Is interred in the cemetery at Lisbon.

HENRY HAVENHILL, Newark, Illinois.

Born in LaSalle county, Illinois, June 17, 1842. Enlisted April, 1861. Discharged for disability April 27, 1862. Died in Chicago, Illinois, of paralysis, June, 1889.

FRANCIS CROWELL, Newark, Illinois.

Born in Tompkins county, New York. Enlisted April, 1861, at the age of eighteen years. Was wounded in the Georgia campaign July, 1864. Mustered out July 16, 1865. Died at Waterman, Illinois, of a complication of diseases, September 17, 1889. The address of his widow is Mrs. Mary A. Crowell, Waterman, Illinois.

THOMAS GARNER.

April, 1861-July 14, 1864. Born in England. Had been a British soldier, and saw active service in the Crimean war. Deserted from the British army. Captured and branded with letter D. Deserted again in Canada and succeeded in escaping to the United States.

Thomas Garner was one of the best marchers and fighters in the Union army. He was always at his post. Never straggled from the ranks and never failed because of sore feet or anything else. Whenever there was fighting on hand Tom was in it. His great failing we all know, but, notwithstanding that, he was the best beloved man in Company K. Some years after the war he went back to England and, in time, returned again to the United States. Soon after his return he walked from Buffalo, New York, to Morris, Illinois, and then came to Newark and Sheridan looking for Company K folks. He found none and went away very despondent. These facts I learned from his friends in Morris. I have received a communication from the Pension Agent at Buffalo, New York, which informs me that Thomas Garner, Company K, 20th Illinois Regiment, was on the rolls of that agency as a pensioner at the rate of six dollars a month, and that he died during the year 1892. He drew pension to July 4 of that year. His address at that time was No. 58 Commercial Street, Buffalo, New York. This is the most definite information I have succeeded in obtaining.

WILLIAM MINARD, Oswego, Illinois.

Born at Walbrough, Ulster county, New York, September 26, 1840. Enlisted May, 1861. Became Commissary Sergeant of the Regiment. Mustered out July 14, 1864. Died at Chicago, Illinois, of disease of kidneys, January 10, 1894. Interred at Graceland.

GEORGE CONNELLY.

May, 1861-September 8, 1862. Born in Ireland. Had been a soldier in the regular army. Was a brave man. Was wounded at Shiloh. Was discharged on account of wound and pensioned therefor. He is now dead. Date of death not ascertained.

JAMES HAGARDORN.

Enlisted at Joliet in May, 1861, and, I think, served about a year and a half. Was discharged for disability and became a pensioner. After the war lived in State of New York. Is now dead. Date of death not ascertained.

JAMES LORD.

May, 1861-March 5, 1863. Was an actor. Came to Newark, Illinois, in the spring of 1861 with a theatrical troupe and there enlisted in Company K. He was a very intelligent man and a good soldier. Was wounded at Fort Donelson. Was discharged for disability and became a pensioner. He is now dead. Date of death not ascertained.

RALPH PRATT.

May, 1861-November 27, 1861. Discharged for disability. Became a pensioner. Is now dead. Date of death not ascertained.

REMARKS.

The names of those who served thirty days with Company K in the State service but who declined to join the Company for three years in the United States service do not appear in this roster; neither do the names of drafted men and substitutes who were assigned to the Company during the last few months of the war.

The dates after a name indicate the time when the soldier first volunteered and the time when he was mustered out or discharged. Those who did not enlist for a second term of three years were nearly all mustered out July 14, 1864. Those who re-enlisted were mustered out July 16, 1865, on account of the close of the war. Those discharged at other dates were discharged for disability resulting from wounds or sickness.

The names of 108 Company K men are herein given; 56 are living, 52 are dead. 4 are missing; of these four I have not been able to obtain any information whatever. I know not whether they are living or dead.

Of the 56 men living, 41 receive pensions; 7 receive no pension. In regard to the others, it is not ascertained whether they are pensioners or not. 32 receive pensions for disabilities incurred in the army; 9 for disabilities not incurred in the army.

Of the 56 men here reported as living, 23 at least were wounded in battle; 13 draw pension for wounds.

Eight Company K men were buried at Raymond—Shoger, Barrows, Waters and Mitchell were buried in the same grave with others of the Regiment on the battlefield, near the rail fence. Adams was buried near the field hospital. Taylor, Reed and Woodruff were buried in the graveyard near the town. Crellen and Wann were buried on the battlefield of Shiloh. None of these graves are now marked or known.

For courtesy, and for information furnished to assist me in tracing lost members of Company K, I am under special obligations to the Hon. WILLIAM LOCHREN, Commissioner of Pensions, Washington, D. C. I also acknowledge my indebtedness to many postmasters, to newspaper editors, to pension agents and others.

If any Company K man dies or changes his place of residence I desire to be informed of the fact. In this way we will know where every man of the Company is located. Remember, please.

A more lengthy sketch is given of some Comrades than of others. The reason is I have had more information in regard to some than in regard to others. In many cases what is said about each one of the living is his own letter to me re-cast and abridged. I have not intentionally slighted or misrepresented any. I may have made errors. If so, I hope they are few and not of a grievous nature.

A BIT OF HISTORY.

When the news of the President's first call for volunteers reached Newark the people were wild with excitement. "That night," writes Dr. Dyer, "I could not sleep. The next morning I was out very early. I went into Fowler's drug store and there with pen and ink drew up a company muster-roll and signed it, and united with others in calling a war meeting for that evening. I was called to make a long ride in the country and upon my return found five names on the muster-roll in addition to my own. I wish I had that paper now." This was the beginning of our Company. Volunteers continued to come forward and in a few days the requisite number had signed the roll. April 24, 1861, is on record as the date of our Company organization. We were not accepted under the President's call and were sorely disappointed. However, most of the boys continued to meet in Newark and were drilled by Lieutenants Watson and McKean. On May 11, 1861, our Company left Newark for Joliet and went into camp. The 20th Illinois Regiment was there organized and the Kendall county boys became Company K of that organization. After that the history of the Company became part of the history of the Regiment. June 13, 1861, we were mustered into the United States service for three years, if not sooner discharged. About the 17th of June we took the cars for the South. Stopped three weeks at Alton, Illinois, and drilled constantly. Early in July we went into camp for a short time in the United States Arsenal at St. Louis, Missouri, and were here armed with Enfield rifles and received new blue uniforms. We now had a very extravagant opinion of ourselves, of our fighting qualities in particular, and did not take the least pains to conceal that opinion from others. This is what a St. Louis paper said of us:

ARRIVAL OF COLONEL MARSH'S REGIMENT FROM ALTON.

At 11 o'clock a. m., of Saturday, the steamer, "City of Alton," from Alton, landed at the Arsenal the Twentieth Illinois Regiment, Colonel C. C. Marsh commanding. The boat brought also the entire camp equipage and stores of the Regiment. The spontaneous greeting tendered by our Missouri soldiers was hearty and enthusiastic. Cheers upon cheers of welcome rent the air and were responded to by the Illinoisans in magnificent style. The guests were assigned the western lawn of the Arsenal grounds for their camping site. Tents were speedily pitched, baggage distributed, and the newly arrived volunteers were soon perfectly at home. They are aching for active service wherever desired, and, we understand, are already under orders for "a forward movement." Other Regiments in Illinois are also in eager anticipation of lively "business" in Missouri or Arkansas.

Colonel Marsh's Regiment is evidently in first-class condition and consists of strikingly vigorous and hardy men. They are brim full of health and energy and fun. The Regiment numbers nine hundred and sixty-one men rank and file. Success and joy to them.

We left the Arsenal in a few days and for six months were engaged in "business" in southeast Missouri. On October 21 we met the Confederates in force, under Jeff. Thompson, at Fredericktown and succeeded in thoroughly convincing them that they were whipped.

February 6, 1862, we entered Fort Henry and ten days later marched in triumph into Fort Donelson. April 6 and 7 we had position in the Union lines at Shiloh and after that took a hand in the siege of Corinth. September 1 were engaged in the sharp little battle of Britton's Lane. In the winter of 1862-3 were in the campaign in the mud in northern Mississippi. Were at Oxford when General VanDorn took Holly Springs and burned our supplies. In the spring and summer of 1863 we participated in all the battles of the Vicksburg campaign and in the siege of that stronghold.

Were out on the Meridian expedition for twenty-nine days in the month of February, 1864, without tents or other protection from the elements except what every man carried on his back.

In the spring and summer of 1864 were in the Georgia campaign and siege of Atlanta. In the fall went from Atlanta to the sea.

In 1865 was in the campaign in the Carolinas and marched through Virginia to Washington after the Confederate armies had surrendered.

On the 16th of July, 1865, at Louisville, Kentucky, the Twentieth Regiment Illinois Volunteer Infantry was mustered out of the United States service and disbanded, and the boys went home.

INDEX.

Lector House believes that a society develops through a two-fold approach of continuous learning and adaptation, which is derived from the study of classic literary works spread across the historic timeline of literature records. Therefore, we aim at reviving, repairing and redeveloping all those inaccessible or damaged but historically as well as culturally important literature across subjects so that the future generations may have an opportunity to study and learn from past works to embark upon a journey of creating a better future.

This book is a result of an effort made by Lector House towards making a contribution to the preservation and repair of original ancient works which might hold historical significance to the approach of continuous learning across subjects.

HAPPY READING & LEARNING!

LECTOR HOUSE LLP
E-MAIL: lectorpublishing@gmail.com